If you were an
INCH or a
CENTIMETER

by Marcie Aboff

illustrated by Sarah Dillard

PICTURE WINDOW BOOKS
Minneapolis, Minnesota

Editors: Christianne Jones and Jill Kalz
Designer: Lori Bye
Page Production: Melissa Kes
Art Director: Nathan Gassman
Editorial Director: Nick Healy
The illustrations in this book were created with watercolor
and gouache.

Picture Window Books
1710 Roe Crest Drive
North Mankato, MN 56003
877-845-8392
www.capstonepub.com

All books published by Picture Window Books
are manufactured with paper containing
at least 10 percent post-consumer waste.

Library of Congress Cataloging-in-Publication Data
Aboff, Marcie.
If you were an inch or a centimeter / by Marcie Aboff ;
illustrated by Sarah Dillard.
p. cm. — (Math fun)
Includes index.
ISBN 978-1-4048-5198-6 (library binding)
ISBN 978-1-4048-5199-3 (paperback)
1. Inch (Unit)—Juvenile literature. 2. Centimeter—
Juvenile literature. 3. Length measurement—Juvenile
literature. 4. Units of measurement—Juvenile literature.
I. Dillard, Sarah, 1961- ill. II. Title.
QC102.A26 2009
530.8'1—dc22   2008037914

Printed in the United States of America in North Mankato, Minnesota.
082011   006231CGVMI

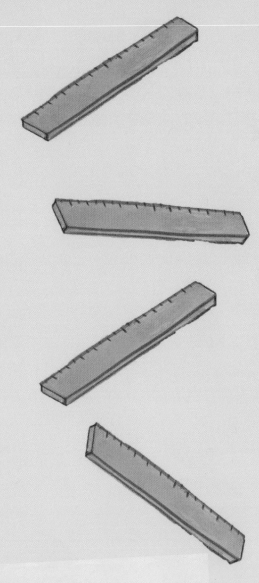

Special thanks to our adviser for his expertise:

**Stuart Farm, M.Ed., Mathematics Lecturer
University of North Dakota**

inch—a unit of English length measurement

centimeter—a unit of metric length measurement

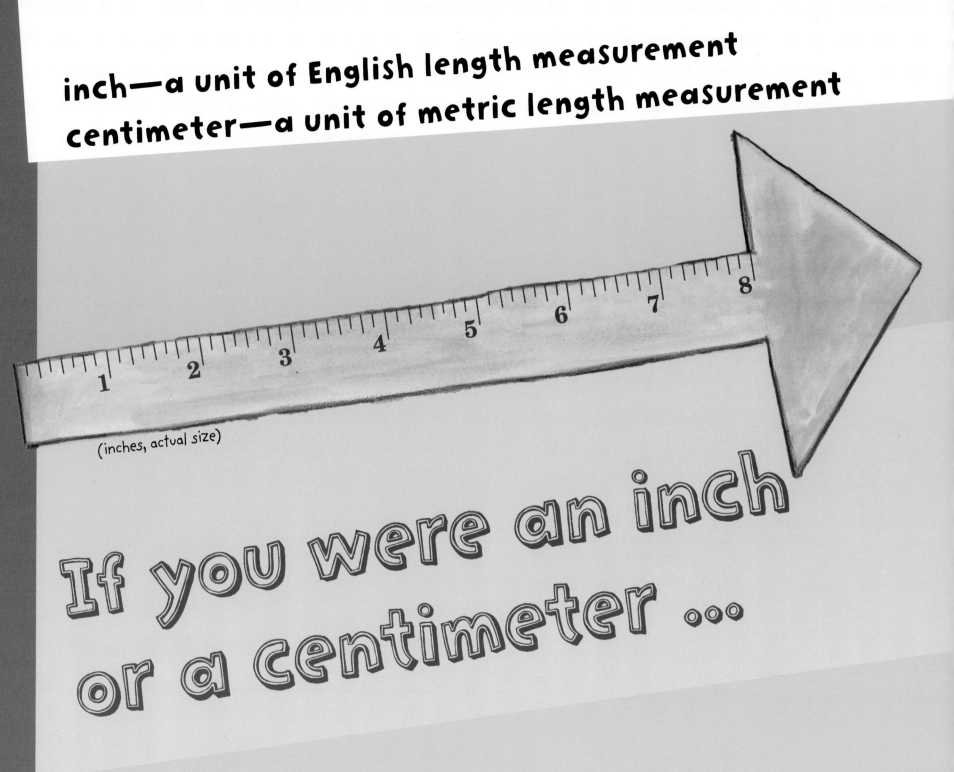

(inches, actual size)

If you were an inch or a centimeter ...

...you could be used in a snowstorm,

on a growth chart,

or on a golf course.

If you were an inch, you would be used to measure things. An inch is part of a foot. Twelve inches equal 1 foot. There would be 12 of you in a ruler and 36 of you in a yardstick.

Dino and Dolly built a new dog house.

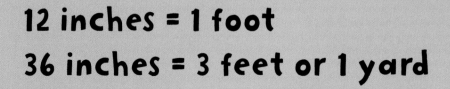

12 inches = 1 foot
36 inches = 3 feet or 1 yard

Dino used a ruler. Dolly used a yardstick.
They both measured a 12-inch window.

7

If you were a centimeter, you would also be used to measure things. A centimeter is part of a meter. There are 100 centimeters in 1 meter.

Sally loved to sew. She sewed 200 centimeters (2 meters) of red fabric, 400 centimeters (4 meters) of blue fabric, and 600 centimeters (6 meters) of yellow fabric.

Her kids loved their new clothes!

100 centimeters = 1 meter

If you were an inch or a centimeter, you could be used in place of one another. In fact, 1 inch equals about 2 and a half centimeters.

"What a messy day, ducks!" the forecaster said. "It rained 2 inches, which means it rained about 5 centimeters."

1 inch = 2.54 centimeters

If you were an inch or a centimeter, you could be shortened. The words *inch* and *inches* can be replaced with the letters *in.* The words *centimeter* and *centimeters* can be replaced with the letters *cm.*

Buzzy missed a home run by only 4 inches.

4 in.

Sammy's soccer ball rolled 10 centimeters inside the goalpost.

10 cm

If you were an inch or a centimeter, people could estimate you by using their thumb. For an adult, the part of the thumb from the knuckle to the top is about 1 inch, or about 2 and a half centimeters. For a child, the entire thumb is about that length.

Victor and his daughter planted vegetable seeds 1 inch, or about 2 and a half centimeters, apart.

Victor used the top part of his thumb
to estimate the distance.
Vicky used her whole thumb.

1 inch

1 inch

If you were an inch or a centimeter, you would be used to measure the width of something. You could describe a television set.

Tex, the TV star, bought a new 72-inch TV set. That's 183 centimeters. What a gigantic sight to see!

72 inches

If you were an inch or a centimeter, you would be used to measure the length of something.

The hairy ape wanted only 2 inches, or about 5 centimeters, of hair cut.

] 2 inches

But the hairstylist had a different idea.
She cut 6 inches, or about 15 centimeters, instead.

Eek!

If you were an inch or a centimeter, you would be used to measure the height of something.

Gina grew 5 inches since her last doctor's visit. She grew nearly 13 centimeters.

THIS YEAR

LAST YEAR

Simon grew 2 inches since his last doctor's visit.

He grew about 5 centimeters.

You would always measure up ...

(centimeters, actual size)

... if you were an inch or a centimeter.

DISTANCE FUN

What you need:

an empty garbage can or bucket
masking tape
a timer
soft balls or scrunched-up paper

a ruler, yardstick, or tape measure
paper
a pen or pencil

What you do:

1. Put the empty garbage can or bucket on the floor.
2. Make a line with the tape and stand behind it.
3. Set the timer for one minute.
4. Try to throw as many balls as you can into the container in one minute.
5. For the balls that don't go in, guess how many inches/centimeters they are away from the basket.
6. Now use a ruler, yardstick, or tape measure to measure the distance.
7. Write down how close you came to the container in inches and centimeters.

NOTE: If you know how many inches you have, you can find out how many centimeters you have, too. Multiply the number of inches you have by 2.54 to get the number of centimeters.

Example: If you have 5 inches, then multiply 5 by 2.54 to get 12.7 centimeters (5×2.54=12.7).

Glossary

centimeter—a unit of metric length measurement, equal to 0.3937 inches

estimate—to guess as close as possible

foot—a unit of English length measurement, equal to 12 inches

inch—a unit of English length measurement, equal to 2.54 centimeters

meter—a unit of metric length measurement, equal to 100 centimeters

ruler—a measuring tool marked off in inches or centimeters

yard—a unit of English length measurement, equal to 3 feet

yardstick—a stick, 1 yard long, used for measuring

To Learn More

More Books to Read

Cleary, Brian P. *How Long or How Wide?: A Measuring Guide.*
    Minneapolis: Millbrook Press, 2007.

Pinczes, Elinor. *Inchworm and a Half.* Boston: Houghton Mifflin, 2001.

Schwartz, David M. *Millions to Measure.* New York: HarperCollins, 2003.

On the Web

FactHound offers a safe, fun way to find educator-approved
Internet sites related to this book.

Here's what you do:

1. Visit *www.facthound.com*

2. Choose your grade level.

3. Begin your search.

This book's ID number is 9781404851986

Index

cm, 12, 13

definition, 3, 6, 8

estimate, 14, 15

foot, 6

height, 20

in., 12

length, 3, 14, 18

meter, 8, 9

ruler, 6, 7, 23

width, 16

yard, 6

yardstick, 6, 7, 23

Look for all of the books in the Math Fun series:

If You Were a Divided-by Sign

If You Were a Fraction

If You Were a Minus Sign

If You Were a Minute

If You Were a Plus Sign

If You Were a Pound or a Kilogram

If You Were a Quart or a Liter

If You Were a Set

If You Were a Times Sign

If You Were an Even Number

If You Were an Inch or a Centimeter

If You Were an Odd Number